ABBEVILLE PRESS PUBLISHERS · 1992

NEW YORK · LONDON · PARIS

STEVEN HELLER & STEVEN GUARNACCIA

PHOTOGRAPHY BY WILLIAM WHITEHURST

ACKNOWLEDGMENTS

Many generous people helped make this book a reality — and a pleasure to do. The authors express their heartfelt appreciation to Johanna Goodman, our principal researcher, whose determination, ingenuity, patience, and good humor made our job all the easier. Sincere gratitude goes to Walton Rawls, our editor at Abbeville Press, who encouraged us to expand the original idea, a book on writing implements ("The Write Stuff"), into this all-encompassing celebration of the American school experience. He also gets an A for his guidance and understanding, and for lending us his National Honor Society medal. ⭐ We are especially grateful to William Whitehurst, our principal photographer, who not only conceived and composed the various tableaux but gave new vigor to some otherwise commonplace material. ⭐ Our deep gratitude goes to Louise Fili and Lee Bearson, the book designers, who organized massive amounts of material, interpreted our ideas into a tangible entity, and gave School Days the perfect visual form. ⭐ We also want to thank the following for their support: Renée Khatami, art director, Ada Rodriguez, studio manager, Hope Koturo, production supervisor, and Robin James, copy chief, all at Abbeville Press; Chris Shipman, Jordin Isip, and Nathaniel Miller for invaluable research assistance; David Spear for his additional photography; Ralph Wernli for his retouching; and Ariel and Jonah Fisher for their crayon renderings. ⭐ If not for the generosity of some avid collectors of school memorabilia this collection would not be as rich: Special thanks to John Craig for a treasure trove of material that we couldn't find anywhere else; Jean Russell for loaning us a plethora of paper ephemera; and Celia Fuller at Abbeville Press for taking her cheerleading uniform out of mothballs just for us. ⭐ For their invaluable help in locating other materials, high marks go to Margot Guralnick, Ed Bourque (superintendent of schools, Fairfield, Connecticut); Linda Mulford and Harriet Gervitz (at the Fairfield Historical Society); Betty Weneck (at the Columbia School of Education, New York); Jerry Harmyk (of U.S.E.D., New York); Diana Epstein (at Tender Buttons, New York); Jacqueline Rea (at the Cooper-Hewitt Museum, New York); Dean Childs and Jackie Saccamano (at the American Automobile Association); Milbrey Jones (at the U.S. Department of Education Research Library); Bernard Riley and Elena Millie (at the Library of Congress); Petrified Films, New York; The Antique Boutique, New York; Little Rickie, New York; Blackbird Antiques, Sheffield, Mass.; folks at The New York Public Library; Myra Frielich, Ray Carroll, Dan Reed, Rick Prelinger, Tom Bodkin, Paul Kopelow, Steven Cohen, Alice Underground, Polly Dufresne, Nancy Haslam, Helene Guarnaccia, Tama Hochbaum, Arthur Adler, Jeff Keedy, Diana Graham, Marcia Lippman, and Susan Hochbaum. ⭐ And an A⁺ to all those who answered our ads for personal material: Harriet Anderson, David Bittner, Myra Boritz, Anne F. Cooper, Harriett Cooper, Kenneth Cooper, Miriam Corbet, Loidian Cordero, Rita W. Dillon, Ken Draya, Stephanie Duchin, Myrna Garber, Mora Johnson, Karl Kraston, Susan Kraus, Naomi Kugler, Yves H. Lacaze, Esther Lafair, Erwin Lerner, Joyce Slayton Mitchell, Mike Mosher, Bill Nave, John Reynolds, Betty Steinhart, Dorothy Snowman, Henry Stone, Linda Trachtman, and Beverly Zingerline. Thanks to Mrs. Spellman, the principal of P.S. 40 in Manhattan, who kept Steven Heller after school twice a week for an entire year. And, last but not least, thanks to the teachers who made Steven Guarnaccia's school days worth remembering, Mary Campbell, Earl Bradley, and J. Paul Toth. —S.H. and S.G.

Editor: Walton Rawls
Designers: Louise Fili and Lee Bearson
Production Supervisor: Hope Koturo

Library of Congress Cataloging-in-Publication Data

Heller, Steven.
    School days/by Steven Heller and Steven Guarnaccia.
        p. cm
    ISBN 1-55859-397-7
    1. Students—United States—Miscellanea. 2. Schools—United States—Collectibles.
    I. Guarnaccia, Steven. II. Title.
LA230.H45 1992
371.8—dc20
                        92-12833
                          CIP

Contents

"School days, school days, dear old golden rule days. . . ." Who can forget the ritual preparations at the end of summer for the first day of school. Remember going to the five-and-dime to buy your supplies? That brand-new loose-leaf binder with the blemish-free, blue-gray cloth covering? The solid ream of white, blue-lined loose-leaf paper you meticulously loaded into that binder? That first red-and-black box of reinforcements, and the individual, multicolored plastic divider tabs? Remember when the adhesive failed and the tab peeled off the very first time the teacher said, "Now, class, turn to the spelling section of your notebooks!" What about first sharpening that box of new Ticonderoga pencils — still without a single chew mark or smudge on the erasers. Or slapping that stiff wooden ruler in the palm of your hand before it got all gashed and crayon-streaked. And pens; so many of them — fountain, cartridge, and ballpoint — to choose from. Parker made the best ballpoint of all, but who could afford the premium price? Bic was the cheapest (and disposable, too), but it could produce unsightly ink blotches on you and the paper and annoying blisters when you held it tightly for too long.

Remember those protective bookcovers for textbooks that you had to fold yourself? Some kids made their own from brown paper bags, but most bought the common, shiny ones with college emblems on them. A few future revolutionaries went after the funny ones with titles like, "School of Hard Knocks," "Sing Sing," and "Alfred E. Newman U," as if sporting these was the most defiant act imaginable. (And speaking of rebellion, remember trying to spell antidisestablishmentarianism, reputed to be the longest word in the English language.) What about the book bag? Some kids preferred a rubber strap with reinforced hooks (which could double as a slingshot), but the best bag was that simulated brown-leather accordianlike briefcase with clasp and combination lock that opened at the top. Inside were three dividers and a little zippered pocket for writing tools. Remember how you carefully and proudly placed your new supplies in their proper sections?

On the first day of school you probably woke up before the alarm. Your mom already had selected your first day's ensemble the night before. ("Mother knows for better clothes it's back to Robert Hall again . . ." was played a lot on the radio in early August to announce the back-to-school season.) Anticipation was high. Who will your new teacher be? How many of the same classmates will you have? The walk or bus ride to school was a great reunion; your pals were just about the same but somehow different, too. You got your locker assignment and went to your new homeroom for the first time, where desks were assigned. If your teacher's name was already written out on the blackboard the incredible suspense was over. Getting a "famous" teacher with a "good reputation" meant that the year would be great. Getting stuck with a "strict" teacher (one who had detention hall written all over her face) signaled disaster. But finding that you drew a new teacher, a young, wet-behind-the-ears, appeared-from-out-of-nowhere teacher, caused you jitters untold. Sizing her up — determining how much or how little you could get away with — was the question of the moment. Of course, there was also the nondescript teacher (neither good nor bad) that you swore to break just because you were sure you could.

Your teacher's introductory remarks revealed a lot about his or her character. A joke put everyone at ease, and talk about plans for the coming year was kind of exciting. But if the riot act was read on that first day — "There will be NO talking, NO gum chewing, and if I catch ANY of you writing on your desk, you will FAIL!" — a difficult ten months was in store.

Textbook distribution was another ritual. A new book was like a tabula rasa; an old one was like wearing a dead man's clothes. Besides putting up with a worn spine and chipped covers, you'd find a roster of the previous owners inside the front cover to which you'd add your own name, or perhaps that of a movie star or president. The previous owners' scribbles, underlines, highlights, and personal marginalia were invariably unwanted distractions. "These books are school property on loan to you. Any student found writing in them will be severely punished!" was every teacher's typical refrain. But after many months, few students took the threat seriously. So you'd write your girl- or boyfriend's name on the edge of the closed book in your own idea of artistic lettering, and for secret inscriptions you'd fan the page edges to make the writing visible only at certain angles. Though most teachers never checked, there was always one who would just happen to be looking over your shoulder at the very moment you decided to make your first scribble.

That first day was also when you'd sign up for the extracurricular stuff. Sports tryouts and the various club, newspaper, and even monitor assignments generated a flurry of excitement. Assuming that the coveted spot on a varsity team was not forthcoming, an appointment as an AAA crossing guard was a plum. As a guard you were entitled to wear the reflective plastic belt with shoulder strap and commanding AAA badge throughout the school day. To please the status seeker, there were also rank gradations (sergeant, captain, etc.) signified by different badge colors. All students were encouraged to take part in an elective activity; the debating, language, drama, music, and civics clubs and the hospitality committee were usually first choices. Your school believed activities built character; your parents assumed they kept you off the streets. Some activities were definitely more prestigious than others; selection for the cheerleading squad was

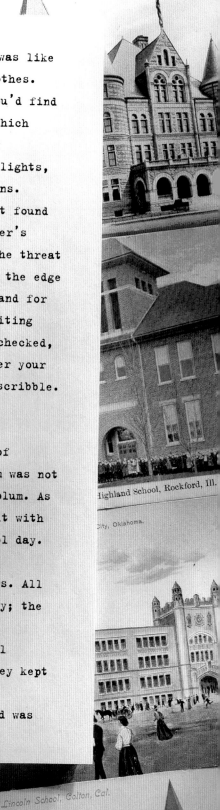

like being awarded a Hollywood movie contract, and appointment (or election) to student government was potentially a quite powerful position. Invariably the shrewdest among you would join the activity for which your teacher served as adviser—an inside track to becoming teacher's pet. Clubs and teams were supposedly for the edification of all, but entry into certain exclusive "honor" societies was by invitation only. Most of the honors were bestowed during the first week of school, and can you ever forget your high anxiety while awaiting the call: inclusion was elevating; exclusion was humiliating.

By the end of the first week, the drill was drilled, the assignments were assigned, and the students were settled in for the long term ahead. Whether one loved or hated school, the months between September and June seemed to last forever. By midterms—those angst-producing examinations—you couldn't wait for Christmas break. And the next eight-week stretch between New Year's and Easter seemed interminable. But after spring recess, the end was finally in sight. By June, once you completed the finals (what a wonderful word!), a school dance or Prom was a well-deserved reward for the year's tribulations.

Sometimes it's hard to believe that over two-thirds of the average American's childhood and adolescence is spent in school. The experience, however, counts among the most formative of your life. How proud you were of your first report card. An "A" or "Excellent" next to your most difficult course was the ultimate validation of hard work. What pride that first varsity letter brought you. What relief you felt after the first class play was over—you never thought that memorizing a few lines could be so difficult! The audience never guessed how many lines you missed. And what about being inducted into the National Honor Society or making the dean's list? Your parents thought you were a genius.

There were major disappointments too: Like not getting the starring role in the play. Or, for an essay you worked so hard on and thought was brilliant, getting only a C⁺ (with added insult written in scarlet ink: "Lazy! You could have developed it further!"). Could it be, you thought, that the teacher had it in for you? Or can you forget the shame of that ignominious parent-teacher conference when your mom and dad learned that you were branded an underachiever. When they returned home that night, summer school was written all over their faces. Of course, the worst moment in any student's life was being sent to detention for transgressing authority, but even more embarrassing was being marched directly to the principal's office for your crime. (How many of you had permanent desks in the principal's office?) With detention there was a slight chance your parents would never find out, but once the principal was involved you might as well kiss your after-school privileges good-bye.

For most of you — with the exception of the lucky ones who skipped or the unlucky ones who were left back a grade — the primary, elementary, and high school experience started after kindergarten and lasted twelve years. Although you never thought so at the time, those years just flew by. For some of us they are best forgotten; for others they figure among their best experiences. Curiously, memories of one's school days tend to be either overwhelmingly good or bad; no one is indifferent to that period in life. Which accounts for why so many of us return decade after decade to their class reunions, or why so many keep souvenirs and mementoes of school days forever. School Days is a scrapbook of these treasures, borrowed from hundreds of former school kids. Most of these artifacts are from public elementary and high schools and span one hundred years of school experience, representing a visual legacy of American education. Personal memories are vividly and poignantly conjured by these keepsakes. The yearbooks, varsity letters, scholarship and citizenship medals, prom cards, and programs form a composite iconography common to all who ever attended grade school, whether urban or rural, north, east, south, or west.

Even with close to a thousand individual pieces, School Days tells only a partial story. A precise inventory of American school ephemera dating just from the end of the nineteenth century, when free, tax-supported public schools were guaranteed to all by law (in most states), would fill hundreds of books this size. Along with the "hornbook" (the colonial child's first lesson book) and the New England Primer, which was published for many years beginning in the late seventeenth century, there were to come countless other primers, readers, spellers, textbooks, tablets, and notebooks. The myriad issues of school newspapers, magazines, and yearbooks would overflow a town library. Likewise, the incredible number of decorative band uniforms would burst a warehouse, as would the distinctive sports uniforms and insignia still made in prodigious numbers. Hence, this Recollectibles volume can offer only a sampling of the curios and memorabilia that touch chords of recognition in former students who want to remember those halcyon (or, for some, tempestuous) school days.

—Steven Heller and Steven Guarnaccia

metic Test Monday

3. By kissing.

4. Animals may spread disease human beings.

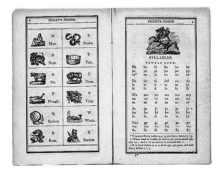

PAUL KOPELOW

THE PREMIER PRIMER

That a picture is worth 10,000 words is one reason why most school primers are so thin. Teaching reading and writing, and learning to distinguish letterforms, is very efficient when images help do the job.

15

I BEFORE E, 'CEPT AFTER C

In 1682 the Proprietor of Pennsylvania decreed that all twelve-year-olds in the province "be instructed in reading and writing..." and taught a useful trade or skill so that "the poor may work to live, and the rich if they become poor may not want."

POSITION FOR READING.

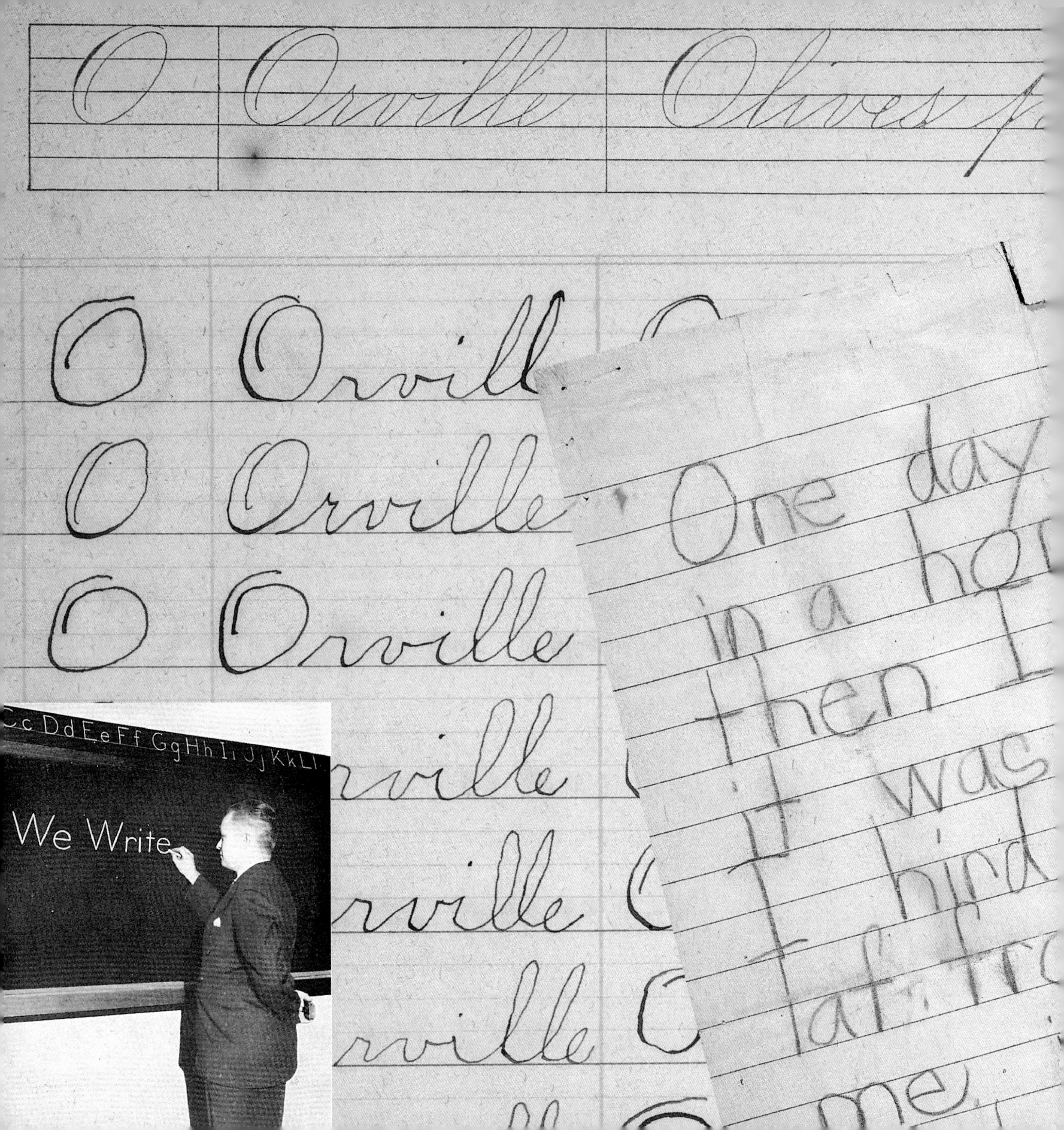

O	Orville	Olives f...

O O Orvill...

O O Orville

O O Orville

...rville

...rville

...rville

One day
in a ho...
then I
was
...hird
af ...
me

We Write

Cc Dd Ee Ff Gg Hh Ii Jj Kk Ll

THE PERFECT HAND

Good penmanship is the mark of a good student. Indeed so many writing systems have been developed—The Palmer Method, The Spencerian System, The Payson, Dunton & Scribner's National System—that keenness for the perfect hand is like questing for the Holy Grail.

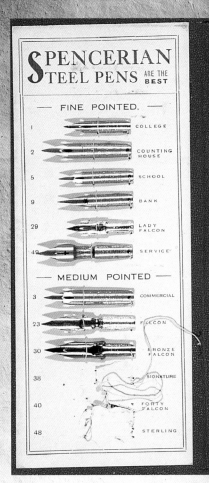

SPENCERIAN STEEL PENS ARE THE BEST

FINE POINTED.

1		COLLEGE
2		COUNTING HOUSE
5		SCHOOL
9		BANK
29		LADY FALCON
49		SERVICE

MEDIUM POINTED

3		COMMERCIAL
23		FALCON
30		BRONZE FALCON
38		SIGNATURE
40		FORTY FALCON
48		STERLING

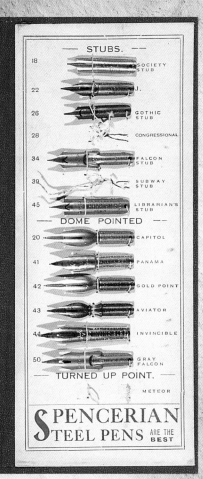

STUBS.

18		SOCIETY STUB
22		J.
26		GOTHIC STUB
28		CONGRESSIONAL
34		FALCON STUB
39		SUBWAY STUB
45		LIBRARIAN'S STUB

— DOME POINTED —

20		CAPITOL
41		PANAMA
42		GOLD POINT
43		AVIATOR
44		INVINCIBLE
50		GRAY FALCON

— TURNED UP POINT. —

		METEOR

SPENCERIAN STEEL PENS ARE THE BEST

LINE FOR LINE

To be well-equipped, a student needed all the right tools. For perfect Spencerian script, what was more important than the right pens and inks? And to get things straight, what was more necessary than rulers, many of them provided as advertising premiums.

THE WRITE STUFF

In 1910 more than twenty million pencils were sold, most to school children. Not surprisingly the major manufacturers advertised their wares directly to children.

TICONDEROGA

A FINE AMERICAN PENCIL WITH A FINE AMERICAN NAME

Ticonderoga Boy

JAMES YEX GROCERY STORE
Prices Right
Right in Your Neighborhood
Groceries - Meats
General Merchandise
Collinsburg, Pa.

LITHO IN U.S.A. P5-4x

DIXON'S ELDORADO

The Master Drawing Pencil

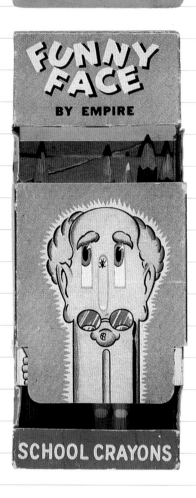

FUNNY FACE

BY EMPIRE

SCHOOL CRAYONS

CHILDS

No. 336.
DIXON'S
COLORED CRAYONS
For Map Drawing.
ONE EACH OF
LIGHT BLUE.
BROWN.
GREEN.
YELLOW.
DARK BLUE.
RED.

Jos. Dixon Crucible Co.
JERSEY CITY, N.J., U.S.A.

No. 7 M TRADE MARK 7 COLORS
MUNSELL CRAYOLA
Patents Copyrights
PURPLE
FIVE PRINCIPAL HUES AT MIDDLE VALUE
AND MIDDLE CHROMA
WITH MIDDLE GRAY AND BLACK
MADE IN U.S.A. EXCLUSIVELY BY
BINNEY & SMITH CO. NEW YORK

MARVEL ART COLORS

WAX POETIC

Binney and Smith Co. introduced its first series of Crayola crayons in 1903. In those days being nontoxic was not at issue. Though Crayola is now synonymous with crayon, scores of manufacturers have produced competing brands.

No 16
SAMMIES
TRADE MARK REGISTERED
SIX COLORED CHALK
CRAYONS

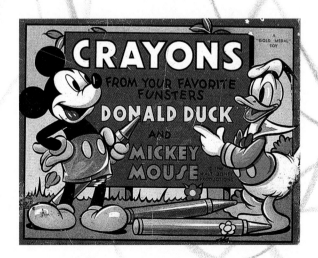

CRAYONS
FROM YOUR FAVORITE FUNSTERS
DONALD DUCK AND MICKEY MOUSE

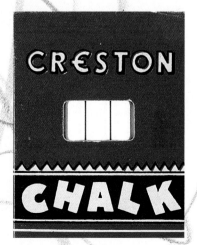

CRESTON CHALK

PENCIL CASE FOR
Eager Beavers

BOXES AND BAGS

Getting just the right pencil box was almost as important as having the best book bag. Though each had humble beginnings—a plain box and a canvas bag—novelty versions have been popular since they were introduced before the Great Depression.

COMPOSITIONS

NAME

MADE IN U.S.A.

THE GREAT TABLETS

In the late 1880s the first bound copybook (followed shortly by the familiar composition book with marbleized cover) made it easier for students to save and retrieve lessons.

HIGH SCHOOL

LITERATURE IS AN AVENUE TO GLORY

NOTE BOOK

Property of

MADE IN U.S.A.

The Red Jacket

SCHOOL SERIES

Spelling Blank

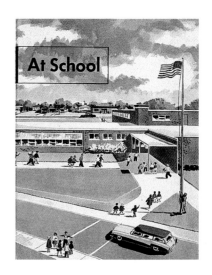

SEE JANE READ

In 1850 an advertisement for "The Phonetic Advocat" promised that "the tedious process of learning to read is rendered speedy and pleasant." Since then thousands of books have been designed to improve the process of deciphering written language.

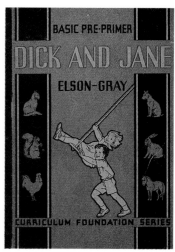

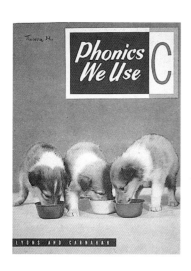

Dick

THE WORLD WE LIVE IN

When the first public schools were established, geography was not one of the subjects taught. It was well into the nineteenth century before physical and world geography were added to the curriculum.

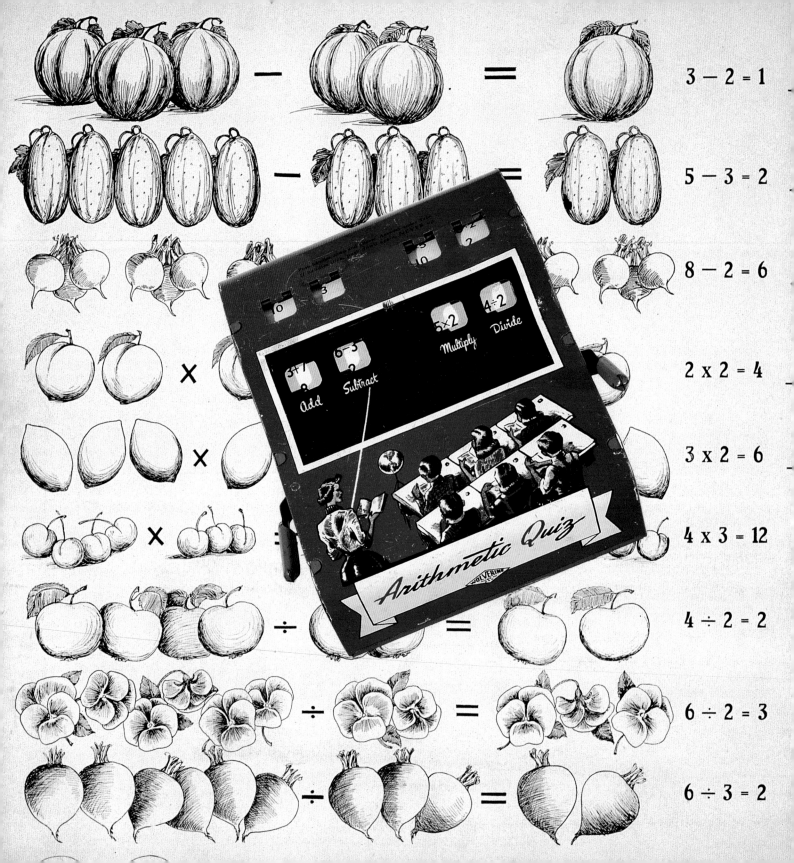

$$3 - 2 = 1$$

$$5 - 3 = 2$$

$$8 - 2 = 6$$

$$2 \times 2 = 4$$

$$3 \times 2 = 6$$

$$4 \times 3 = 12$$

$$4 \div 2 = 2$$

$$6 \div 2 = 3$$

$$6 \div 3 = 2$$

Arithmetic Quiz

OLD DIVISION, NEW MATH

The third "r," 'rithmetic, once called "ciphering," was not (according to early school officials) as important to the well-rounded student as reading and spelling were until well into the nineteenth century. But, today, can you imagine not knowing the sum of two plus two?

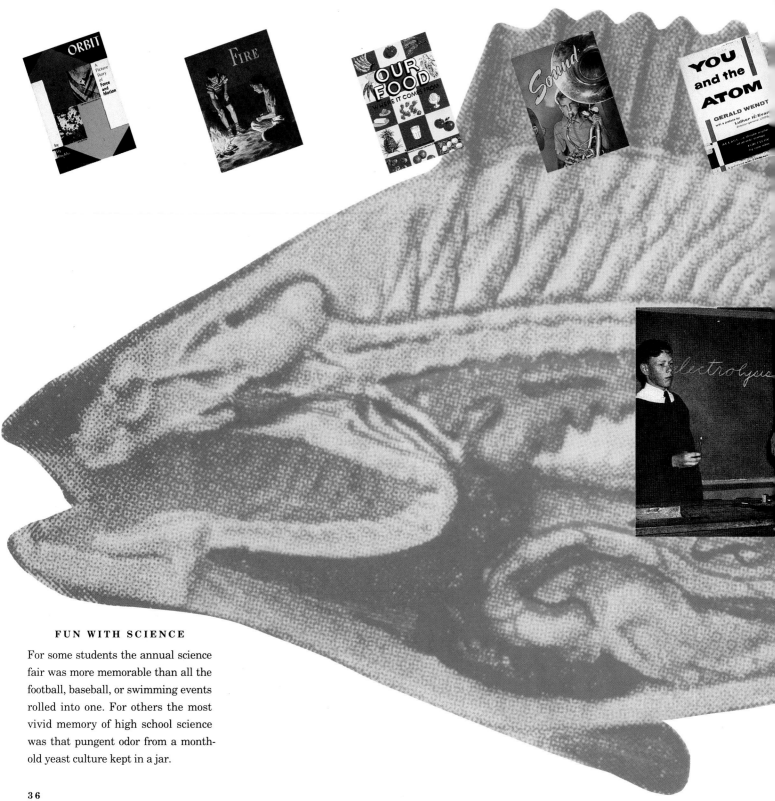

FUN WITH SCIENCE

For some students the annual science fair was more memorable than all the football, baseball, or swimming events rolled into one. For others the most vivid memory of high school science was that pungent odor from a month-old yeast culture kept in a jar.

Hallowed Halls

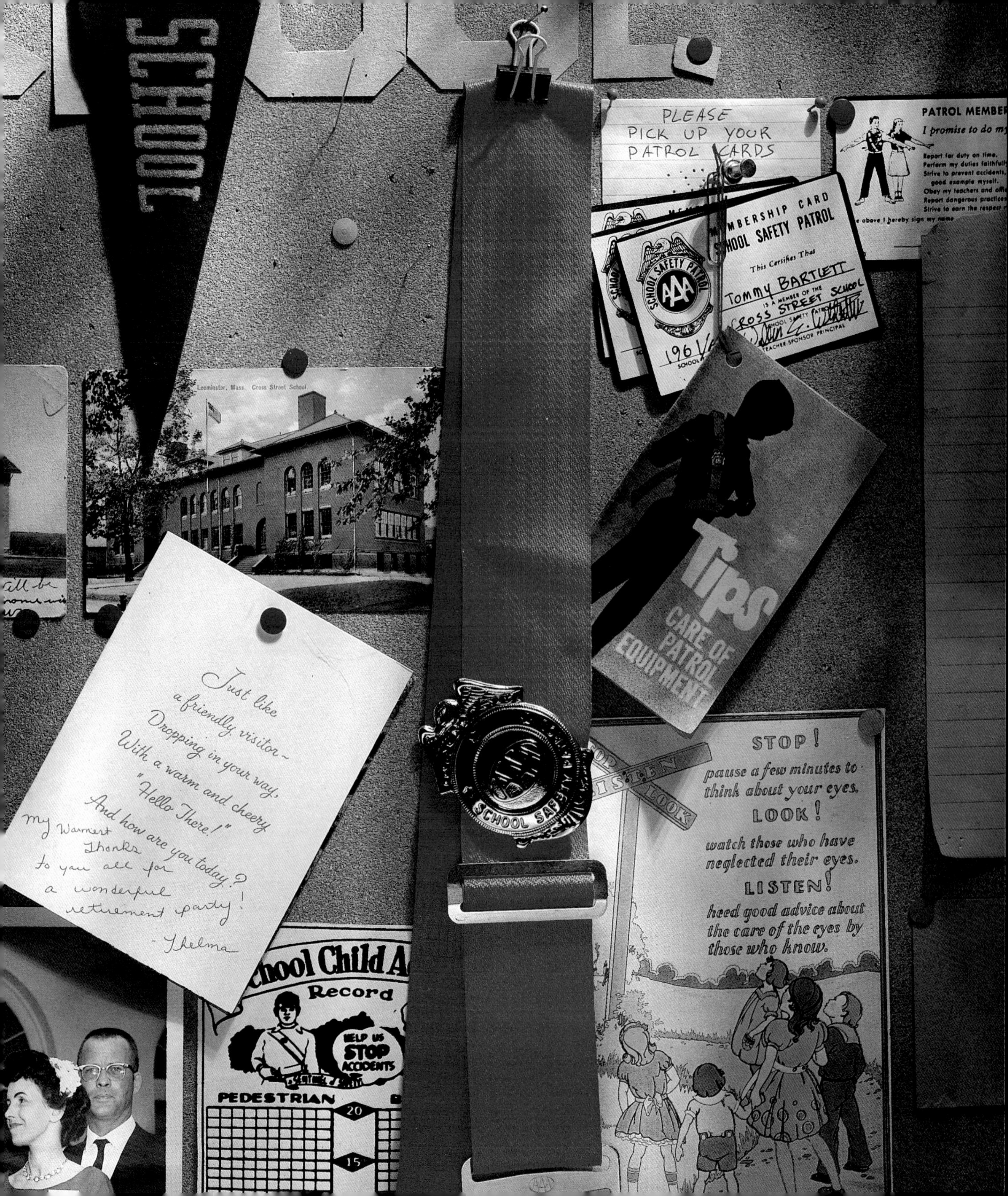

Grasmere School

Lincoln School

Former Sherman School

Oldfield School

Mill Plain Elementary School

Nathan Hale School

Pequot School

Holland Hill School

Bancroft School

Jefferson School

Fairfield Woods School

Former Sherman School

Dwight School

Fairfield High School

Dwight School

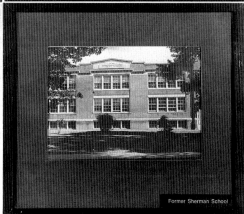

Former Sherman School

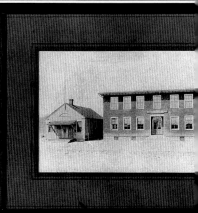

1 RM., BLACK BD. VU

In colonial times most schoolhouses were crude and uncomfortable, often roofed with bark and unheated. Children whose parents did not supply firewood were kept farthest from the fire.

Lafayette School

Stratfield School

McKinley School

McKinle

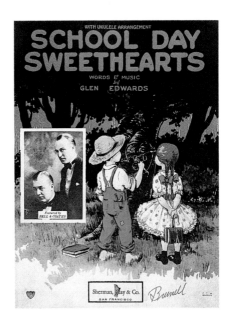

School - days,   school   days,   dear old go

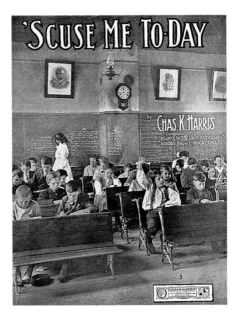

SCHOOL BALLADS

Everyone knows the words and tune to Cobb & Edwards's famous old song "School-Days." However, it was just one of many published songs devoted to memories of what were surely the best days of our lives.

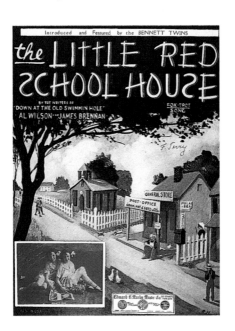

n rule - days

FREE LUNCH

Chop suey, American cheese sandwich, canned peas, Jell-O mold, and, for some, ketchup as a vegetable: The school lunch. The cafeteria kitchen was, neverthless, a place of culinary mystery.

1 DRINK ~8~ GLASSES OF WATER DAILY

2 MILK GIVES... HE...

3 BRUSH

4 Walk for Health

5 NINE HOURS FOR SLEEP

FIRE IS A DANGEROUS PLAYTHING

BATHE OFTEN

7 EAT VEGETABLES

WAL... FO... HEALT...

Help Yourself to Good Teeth

Department of Health — City of New York

9 WEAR YOUR RUBBERS

HEALTHY MINDS AND
HEALTHY BODIES

No one was more benevolent than the
school nurse. She taught us the right
way to brush, the best foods to eat,
and wrote the note that released us
from school when we were sick.

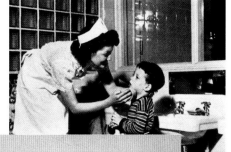

Board of Education
of the City of New York

Health Certificate of Merit

Harriet Gevirtz

has given satisfactory evidence of practicing the rules for good health
and personal hygiene; has made regular gain in height and weight;
drinks plenty of milk each day and eats the right kinds of food.

IN TESTIMONY WHEREOF we have affixed our signatures
hereto this _____ day of _May_, 1936

Public School No. 62 Borough B'k'n

P. Banks
TEACHER

Harold G. Campbell
SUPERINTENDENT OF SCHOOLS

A.S. Karscher
PRINCIPAL

The
HEALTHY
SCHOOL CHILD

*Massage your gums every time
you brush your teeth*

incognito
imperative
invigorate
invalid

$= 48$
$= 54$
$= 60$
$= 66$
$= 72$

HEY, TEACH!

Teachers have been characterized as spending 12 hours a day searching for truth, and the other 12 hours searching for error. Perhaps *more* remarkable, a teacher is someone who likes someone else's children.

WHY IS THE SKY BLUE?

WHY IS RAIN DIRTY?

WHAT IS THE HIGHEST WATERFALL IN THE U.S.?

CAN A WHALE DROWN?

IS NIAGARA THE HIGHEST WATERFALL

WHAT IS THE WORLD'S OLDEST LIVING THING?

WHO INVENTED THE WATCH?

HOW MANY RIBS HAVE WE?

LIGHTS, CAMERA, EDUCATE!

Didn't all kids daydream of having their teacher transformed into Sidney Poitier or Doris Day? And how come no one had a teacher like "Our Miss Brooks"?

OARD
GLE

RTLING PICTURE
OF THE YEAR!

THE
BLACKBOARD
JUNGLE
BY EVAN HUNTER

The sensational novel... now on the screen!

ORD
UIS CALHERN

REEN PLAY BY RICHARD BROOKS · BASED ON THE NOVEL BY EVAN HUNTER
S · PRODUCED BY PANDRO S. BERMAN AN M-G-M PICTURE

MONOGRAM PICTURES presents
The Teen Agers JUNIOR PROM

THE STORY OF GRACE MOORE

JELLICOE HIGH SCHOOL
CLASS OF 1917

WARNER BROS. PRESENT   STARRING KATHRYN
"So This is Love"   GRAYSON

CAMPUS
HONEYMOON
A Republic Picture

HOLLYWOOD 101

School has been a popular setting for Hollywood movies ever since school kids first snuck out of class to go see them.

THE TUNE OF A HICKORY STICK

Once corporal punishment was the norm for even minor infractions. The "whispering-stick," a thin green branch that hurt like the dickens, was used for discipline in addition to dunce caps and placards that read "Idle." "All," said the teacher, "for the good of the children."

THE GOOD, THE BAD, AND THE TARDY

Rewards of merit, the flip side of punishment, were frequently handed out to "good" students in the nineteenth century as a way of instilling a sense of pride. Later the report card and other honors for good scholarship replaced these early rewards.

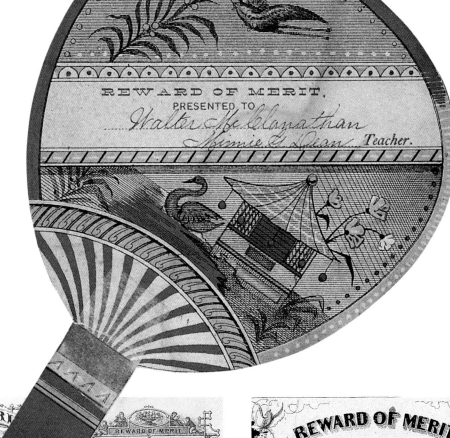

REWARD OF MERIT.
PRESENTED TO
Walter McClanathan
Mimie F. Dean Teacher.

REWARD OF MERIT
Presented to
By Teacher.

REWARD OF MERIT
Presented to Harrie Lindsay
By L. K. Barnes
Aug.

REWARD OF MERIT
Presented to Genealatia,
By Sarah

REWARD OF MERIT
Presented to Bessie
By Evelyn Instruct.

Reward of Merit.
Presented to
By Teacher.

Oh, did the Son of God most high
Consent a man to be;
And did that blessed Saviour die,
Upon the cross, for me?

Accept, O ever blessed Lord,
An infant's humble praise;
Teach me to love thy holy word,
And serve thee all my days.

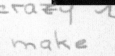

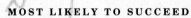

MOST LIKELY TO SUCCEED

For a reasonable fee a publishing company in Topeka, Kansas, would design and print the basic yearbook, but wasn't it more fun to write, decorate, and lay it out yourself?

65

ASSEMBLY LINE

Assembly was the hour-long period every month when math was cancelled so your schoolmates could dress like Union soldiers and sing songs of the Civil War.

ORCHESTRA

Boom! Boom! Boom!
Clang! Clang! Clang!
"Come on, David," said Patty.
"You can play, too."
What are these children doing?

26

MUSIC APPRECIATION

Students who couldn't play instruments played recorders. And those who couldn't play recorders played tonettes, and those who couldn't play tonettes sang "Frères Jacques." But if you had luck and the talent, the glee club or band were extracurricular activities with social cachet.

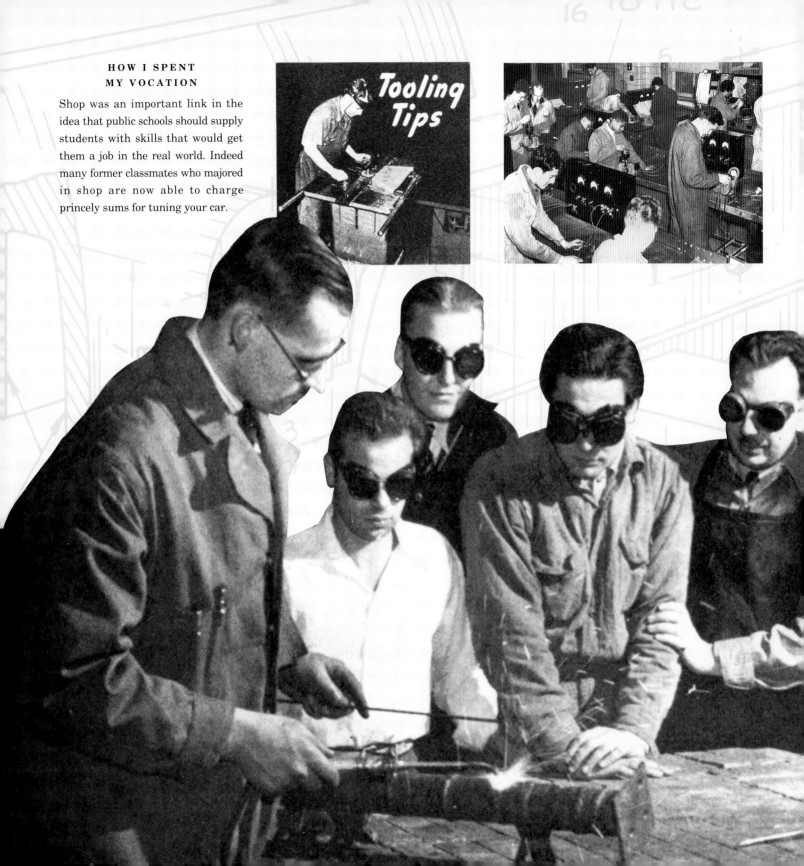

HOW I SPENT MY VOCATION

Shop was an important link in the idea that public schools should supply students with skills that would get them a job in the real world. Indeed many former classmates who majored in shop are now able to charge princely sums for tuning your car.

Tooling Tips

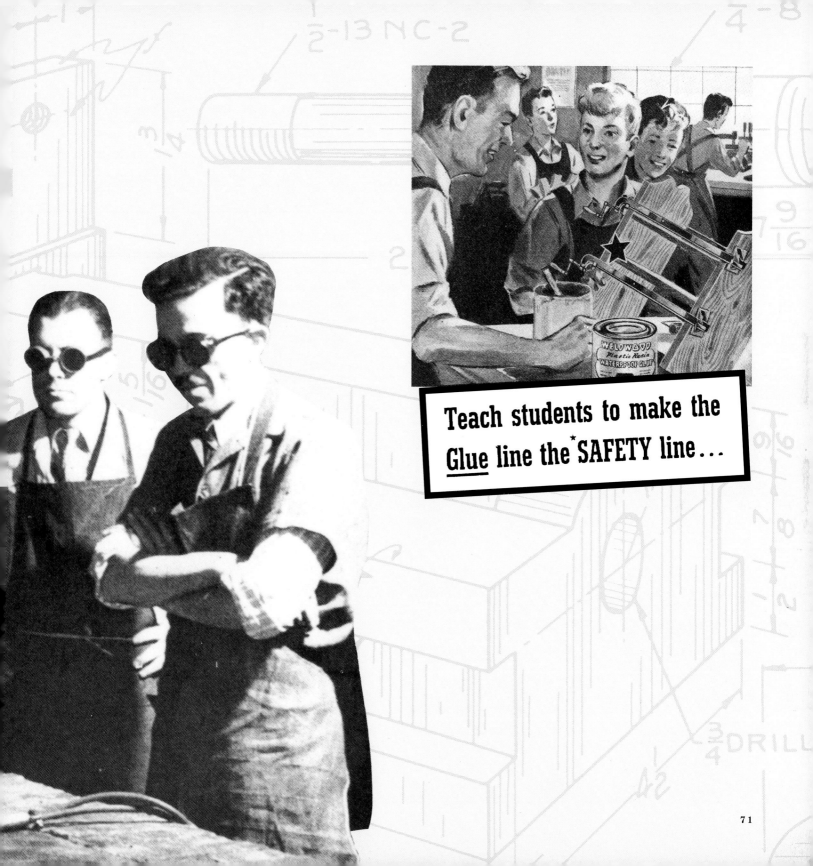

Teach students to make the Glue line the *SAFETY line...

WOMEN'S WORK

Stereotypes were instilled early. Girls were required to take home economics (and typing, too) to prepare the future little woman for life at home—to cook, sew, do laundry, and keep the household records.

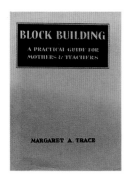

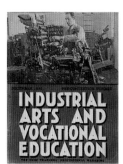

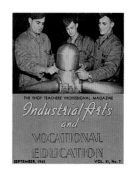

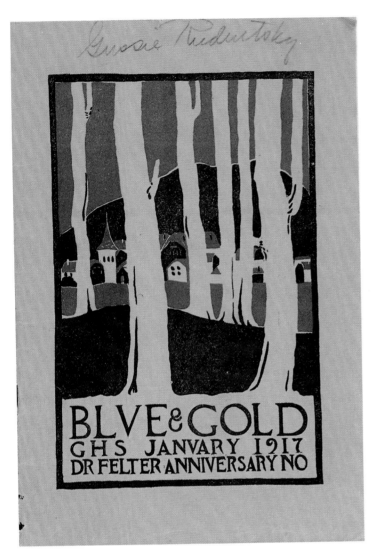

Countless journals about education were aimed at teachers and parents, but only the school paper was written and edited by the students themselves. School papers came in many shapes and sizes, and some were mimeographed while others were professionally printed. These papers were the exclusive voice of the student body; and sometimes, when the supervising teacher was not looking, the hottest news in school was published.

ARTS AND CRAFTS

The number of activities a teacher can devise that include scissors, tasty white paste, and construction paper are infinite. The volume of cut paper produced during the average school year would alone fill a giant landfill.

A Drawing Lesson for Beginners

By ANNE LOUISE PRESTON

The teacher may draw a circle on the blackboard and ask the class to draw one on paper. "What can you make out of one circle?" she asks. The children suggest apple, face, and so on. After these pictures have been made, the teacher may suggest drawing a kitten, rabbit, chicken, and pig. As she draws the pictures on the blackboard, she describes each step in detail. The children may then draw the pictures on paper and color them with crayons or paints.

"Good-bye! ———
Remember, - look both ways
before crossing the street."

SCHOOL
SLOW

SLOW, SCHOOL CROSSING

Hold hands, walk in line, cross at the green; how often were these admonitions repeated? Not suprisingly, the crossing monitor had one of the most responsible posts in school—since he could report any student who didn't obey the rules.

JAMES M. KIERAN 123 JUNIOR HIGH

EAST

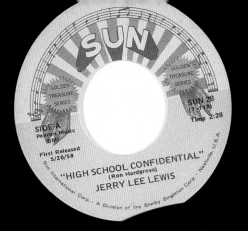

SUN

GOLDEN TREASURE SERIES

GOLDEN TREASURE SERIES

SUN 28
(7 1/8)
Time 2:28

SIDE A
Penron Music
BMI

First Released
5/20/58

Sun International Corp. - A Division of the Shelby Singleton Corp. - Nashville, U.S.A.

"HIGH SCHOOL CONFIDENTIAL"
(Ron Hardgrove)
JERRY LEE LEWIS

ERIC
RECORDS

Arc
Music Corp.
(BMI)
Time: 2:43

225
(E-1974)

SCHOOL DAY
(Ring! Ring! Goes The Bell)
(Chuck Berry)
CHUCK BERRY

ERIC RECORD CO. WESTVILLE, N.J.

CLIFTON
RECORDS

1135 MAIN AVE.   CLIFTON, N.J. 07011
201-365-0049

45-9
(C-109-A)
BMI 2:22

A SCHOOL GIRL IN LOVE
(The Sharmeers)
THE SHARMEERS

ATLANTIC
OLDIES SERIES

45 R.P.M.

ATLANTIC

VOCAL
58C-3040 SP

OS 13055
Pub. Walden-
Tweed ASCAP
Time: 2:08
FROM ATCO
6127

QUEEN OF THE HOP
(Woody Harris)
BOBBY DARIN

MFG. BY ATLANTIC RECORDING CORP. 75 ROCKEFELLER PLAZA, N.Y. N.Y.   A WARNER COMMUNICATIONS COMPANY

ROULETTE

MADE IN U.S.A. BY ROULETTE RECORDS, INC.

GOLDEN GOODIES
HITS SERIES

GG - 59
Frost Music
Corp. BMI

45 RPM
(g 170 bw)

SCHOOLHOUSE ROCK
(Terry-Gordon)
NICKY & THE NOBLES

**HIGH SCHOOL
BANDSTAND**

In the mid-fifties, rock 'n' roll music
was prohibited from anywhere within
earshot of many high schools. Never-
theless, the "animal beat" found its
way into student consciousness
through songs on the radio or in
the movies about high school
life and love.

Parkway
RECORDS, INC.

Lowe Music
ASCAP

Time 2:14

THE CLASS
(Kal Mann)
CHUBBY CHECKER
IMITATING
FATS DOMINO,   THE COASTERS
ELVIS PRESLEY & THE CHIPMONKS
804B

LE 1009

SCHOOL IS OUT
(Anderson-Barge)
GARY (U.S.) BONDS

VARSITY SQUAD

Nothing was more humiliating than suiting up for the game but sitting it out on the bench the entire season. For the stars of football, wrestling, swimming, and the rest, nothing was as sweet as victory—and earning that varsity letter.

VALLEY FORGE JR. HIGH

FREEHOLD TWP. FLAG TWIRLER

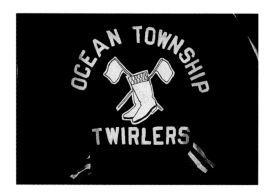

OCEAN TOWNSHIP TWIRLERS

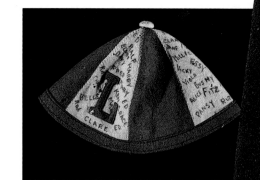

GLOVERSVILLE

UNION HIGH DRILL TEAM

SCHOOL TOGS

What kid wouldn't sacrifice a month of hot lunches for a personalized school jacket. It was not just an item of clothing, it had near religious implications as the reliquary of four years of high school memories.

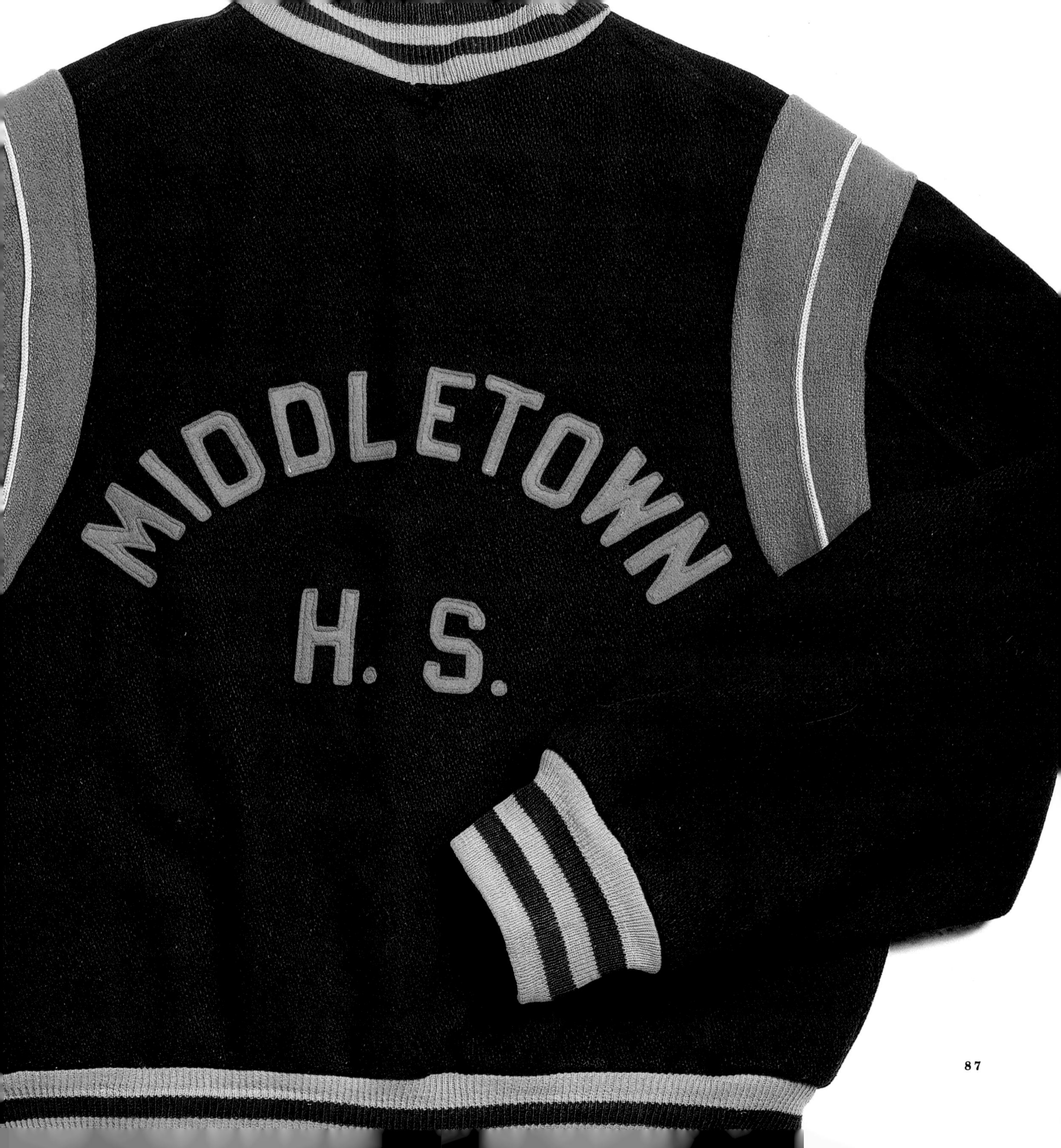
MIDDLETOWN
H. S.

FAIRFIELD WOODS JR. HIGH

THOMAS JEFFERSON SCHOOL

LEARN TO LIVE · LIVE TO LEARN

PENNSBURY HIGH SCHOOL

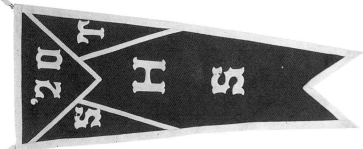

Wyomissing

WYOMISSING HIGH SCHOOL

SOUDERTON AREA HIGH SCHOOL

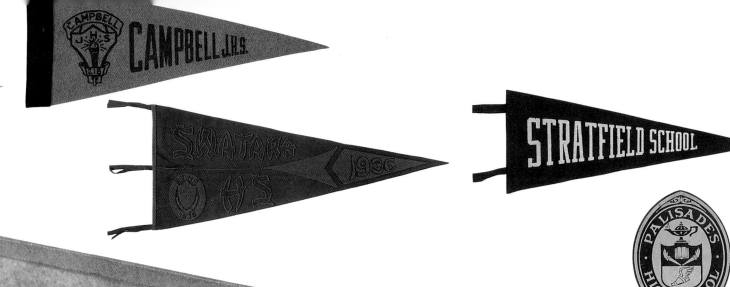

THE BANNER YEARS

Any school worth its name had its own special pennant, or seal, or mascot. But few were unique. Since one supplier usually catered to all the schools in a region, the same basic letterforms and stock images often were repeated.

RAH, RAH, SIS-BOOM-BAH

The most popular girls in school were those select few who learned the cheers, mastered the split, shook the pom-poms with vigor, and cheered the home team on to victory.

GIVES YOU MORE GO

Bond Bread

Judges of dance contest were Under Secretary of State and Mrs. Edward R. Stettinius Jr. (center), whose son Ted (below) is student at the school. A 12-piece band played for the dance.

Ted Stettinius gets tie straightened by Marjory Rhett while his parents chuckle at his discomfort. A shy young fellow, Ted disliked having his picture taken. He did not have a date.

At intermission there was a scamper for comfortable seats in the lounge off the gym, where some of the dateless younger boys were stretched out sleepily. Dance ended at 2 o'clock.

David Schenck, a sixth former, used spoon to demonstrate dance figures for his guest, Betty Nutt of Greensboro, N.C. A special edition of the school paper was delivered at dinner.

Life Goes to a *Junior Dance*

Boys at Woodberry Forest School in Virginia are hosts at "Midwinters"

Most important social event of the year at Woodberry Forest School near Orange, Va. is the Midwinters, a series of parties extending over a weekend following first-semester exams. On this occasion the boys—whose ages range from 12 to 18—ask the prettiest girls for miles around (see essay) to be their guests, and the school puts them up dormitory-fashion in rooms above gymnasium and in the historic "Residence." In this house, designed by Thomas Jefferson for President Madison's brother William, the school was started in 1880 by Captain Robert Stringfellow Walker, C.S.A. His son, J. Carter Walker, is the present headmaster.

An outbreak of measles a month before the appointed weekend threatened to cancel plans for the party, but each invited guest was advised of the situation and was told she was welcome to come at her own risk. Very few refused. Met at the train Friday afternoon by their hosts, the girls were taken on a tour of the grounds, then rested for the formal dinner and dance shown here. Saturday's program included breakfast for Hop committee and their girls at a cabin in the woods owned by one of the masters. A basketball game, tea dance, buffet supper and another formal dance that night brought the Midwinters to a flourishing climax.

LINES MARKING THE BASKETBALL COURT SHOW PLAINLY

ON GYM FLOOR AS THE COUPLES PAIR FOR FIGURE DANCE

STAG LINE CONSISTED MOSTLY OF BOYS WITHOUT DATES.

FACES SHOW MIXTURE OF AWE, BOREDOM, ANTICIPATION

CONTINUED ON NEXT PAGE

Norman Rockwell

92

PROM NIGHT

A rite of passage, the Prom was fraught with teenage tension. Will I have a date? Will my dress be ready on time? Will I find true love? Will my complexion be clear?

FUN AND GAMES

Learning can be fun was the implied message of all the toy, game, and novelty companies that cashed in on the school experience.